# Inspirations from the Heart: Seasons of Change

Pamela G. Rowell-Scoggins

Order this book online at www.trafford.com
or email orders@trafford.com

Most Trafford titles are also available at major online book retailers.

Printed in Victoria, BC, Canada.

ISBN: 978-1-4269-2307-4 (sc)

ISBN: 978-1-4269-2308-1 (dj)

Library of Congress Control Number: 2009913010

*Our mission is to efficiently provide the world's finest, most comprehensive book publishing service, enabling every author to experience success. To find out how to publish your book, your way, and have it available worldwide, visit us online at www.trafford.com*

*Trafford rev. 12/15/2009*

 www.trafford.com

**North America & international**
toll-free: 1 888 232 4444 (USA & Canada)
phone: 250 383 6864 ♦ fax: 812 355 4082

I want to give glory to the Most High God, the only one who deserves the praise and glory for all of this written word.
Thank You, Father!


This book is in memory of Mel Rowell, Jr.
Thank you for all that you've given to me.  What a legacy you've left!
I will always love you. - Pam

I want to thank all of my family and friends who have been so supportive to see this book become a reality.
Thank You Russell for loving me in this new season!  I love you with
all my heart!
Thank you!

Dear Reader,

I want to express my thanks to you for your support through the purchase of this book. I cannot write without the Divine inspiration of God, my Father, who is the only and ultimate source of my inspiration.

I pray that this book will be a blessing and inspiration to each one of you! As you read my poems, let God's grace touch your heart. This book is divided into six parts:

**Family Portraits** – these poems are dedicated to different members of my family.

**Petals of Friendship** – these poems are dedicated to friends that are about the different faces of friendship.

**Unfolding Eternal Love** – these poems are about love between husband and wife, the love ordained by God.

**Fallen Petals of Sorrow** – these poems were written in the deep times of sorrow in my life. Writing these were painful and desperate, but the only way I could express my sorrow.

**Shades of Color** – these are different types and kinds of poems like Christmas poems, Patriotic poems, Sonnets etc.

**Unopened Packages of Hope** - these poems are dedicated to people, who in their situations, were divinely inspired by God as poems of hope and mercy.

My prayer for you, Beloved, is that through this written word you will find God's hope and receive encouragement as you realize His mercy for you! I pray that you will enjoy these words penned from heaven as Inspirations from the Heart!

Pamela G. Rowell-Scoggins

# Contents

# Family Portraits

*Here are hung portraits of faith and love...*
*forgiveness and mercy...an eternal heritage.*

**-Pam Rowell-Scoggins**

# _The Legacy Of Willie Mae Milligan_

For My Grandmother on her Birthday

80 years have come and gone
we celebrate today,
not only for the years gone by,
but as your life remains.

Each of us has grown in years,
you've shouldered many sorrows
and through each one, you've always been
great strength and hope for tomorrow.

Your love, though unconditional,
was tested, tried and proved,
your faith in God stood strong through time
when time was cruel and true.

Your legacy lives on in us
look at each face, you'll see,
the love and faith you've handed down,
passed on for all to be.

You've been our light to lead us to
a path we each must find.
When it is dark, your light will shine
and lead us further on.

# Paw Paw

In Memory of My Grandfather, J.L. Milligan

A man of Irish heritage
from land so lush and green,
his roots, his temper driven down
a rich and steady stream.

His house, he rules with strictest hand,
his love was so demanding,
he gave his heart, his soul, his life
to God, his faith withstanding.

When even life so great a struggle,
he took them all, every hurdle,
into a place where hardness melts
the toughest heart so tender felt.

A promise made, but it was broken
No peace he found in earthly token,
For years, he wrestled in the dark
no light he found from God apart.

On wings of doves with lifted prayer
he gave to God every care.
With new desire in his heart
God gave his life a brand new start.

Now humor lies in deep blue eyes
his ringing laughter heard,
for miles around, you bet you've found
his aggie jokes go 'round.

He tirelessly a fishin',
just waitin' and a wishin'
for just one tug a runnin' he would tell,
of one fish in all it's glory,
an exaggerated story,
a story stretched, his favorite of all tales.

With deeper faith than found before,
Boldly, he proclaimed God's Word,
He preached with strength and deep conviction
Well in his forties, with no restriction.

God called him out and filled him with
compassion, love, caring concern
his life was music, blissful song,
when days were hard and time grew long.

A very strong and Godly man,
a suffering servant in God's plan.
His life was taken up so short,
He gave each one of us a start.

His love, it stays forever near,
our hearts with gladness, rich with cheer.
When thinking back upon his life,
while keeping heaven in our sight.

Then we will know a greater joy,
Than having been on earthly soil,
for on that day, we'll see him there
where Son and light meet in the air.

# Her Shining Light

In Memory of Verna Jo Rowell

She walks in strength as beauty flows
so does her love expressed
it shines with light from up above
straight down into your heart.

This light, its source and common course
have reached with equal grace
a place where pride meets selflessness
tenacious, unafraid.

Historically, a road winds down,
her feet are made to walk,
but watch her steps
a path she takes into a greater dawn.

Protective hand placed down upon
the ones she loves so dear
she never wanders far from home
but keeps forever near.

So as the road meets at the cross
so life and light leads on
to a place we each must go
a country far beyond.

But this is not the end, you see,
her life means so much more.
The road, the path, the place she walks
is never far to roam.

Look out, you'll see her footsteps lead
to a path you'll soon discover,
where hardships free, a place to be
She chose the road less traveled.

# Thelma Louelle

In loving memory of Granny Rowell

A sweet angelic face set 'round,
Her hair, light, fluffy white,
brown eyes that shine with beauty bright,
rich laughter there is found.

Pure heart of gold, rich depths of love,
for only God alone.
She lived her life, tenderhearted,
within His Word to grow.

Great love of sports,
held out last resort for her favorite team,
when they won, her face would beam
with victory it would seem.

She was so wise beyond her years,
she calmed a heart, relieved great fears,
she'd always know the answer for
a problem, at your heart had torn.

Her legacy is born in us,
great faith on which to stand,
rich heritage to place your trust,
she rests within the Master's hands.

So, choose this day what path to take
the highest call is now at stake.
Her footprints lead through trials deep
for down the narrow road is steep.
She could see the old rugged tree
where the Son of God did bleed,
no greater love will ever be,
this sacrificed Lamb of eternity.

Here lies the hope she left for you,
a gift that's free, forever true
with all her heart, she longed to see,
the love of God flow through you and me.

# _Mom_

For Jo

Mom says, "Don't cry for me – I'm always there".
She was proud and stubborn, but her stick to it
perserverance was her strength.  She was a fighter that loved hard and
filled my stomach because she was a good cook.
MMM!  Banana Pudding!  Deviled Eggs!
Great food – great love – great strength
that spoke compassion in everything she did,
everyone she touched, everywhere she was…


MOM!

# Evening at the Beach

I felt the grit between my toes as ocean liners passed,
seagulls squawked and cawed
giving the teenagers having a party an audience.
As I stepped and stooped for seashells,
skittering crabs were going toward the foamy water.
The fire by the ocean lit the night with an orange glow.

# *He Gave Me the Best*

For My Mom

What can I say, how can I tell you,
All that's in my heart?

You carried me, held me, in times of great need
even when I couldn't see.

You lovingly nurtured, our lives intertwined,
many times, my life caused you grief.

Through turbulent times, you held onto me
when my life was topsy turvy.

Yesterday's gone, tomorrow's not sure
we only have this moment true.

I am so thankful for all of life's trials
lessons learned extend now for miles.

Your love shaped my life with many great things
that only a good Mother brings.

I'm thankful to God for when it comes to Mom's,
He reached down and gave me the best!

# *Daddy's Little Girl*

A little girl whose world revolved 'round Daddy's love to be,
she longed for him to hold her close with abandoned world carefree.
At nine years old, dealt life's cruel blow, he broke her heart, you see,
for Daddy could not give his love, hatred's head reared black and ugly.
Her childlike heart built thickened walls no love could break them
down, when she grew up she felt so small,
no hope or courage could be found.
With nothing more at stake, she tried her life to take,
she cried through silent years gone by, not wanting to survive.
So many mistakes she made, high consequences paid,
her soul in deep despair, she labeled life unfair.
Rejected, ruined, lost, her marriage was the cost,
She reached the darkest depths, her hope there was none left.
Tears flowed down cheeks unchecked while life, she did reflect,
God reached within her soul, He radically made whole.
Where once was hatred, love abides,
forgiveness borne, when released her pride,
"I love you Daddy, always know, even when your love's not shown."
A broken vessel, He transformed,
where once was darkness, light was borne,
determined, she would overcome,
her fear relinquished to the Son.
God spared her life persistently,
as Jesus hung on Calvary's tree,
her sin to conquer, His love is free,
receive God's gift, eternity.
So, now, my friend, submit and yield,
for God will all your dreams fulfill,
when you have placed Him in your heart,
He'll give your life a brand new start.
God's grace and mercy fresh each day,
He is the potter, I am the clay.
Please impart God's heart within,
that I may run the race to win.

# *My Dream Is Real*

To Mel

My heart is soaring lighter than air,
My love for you cannot compare
To how I cherish you.

There are no jewels, you are rare,
nor is there beauty that would so dare,
To shine my love for you.

My heart, you captured, it is yours,
my soul enraptured with love so pure,
To give you all I have.

A single moment has not ticked,
where I've forgotten, you have picked,
To love me always.

Our love began some years ago,
was planted, watered, it was foretold,
To give God greatest glory.

Now, my love, I tell you this,
no one can measure nor give greater bliss,
To you alone, I cling.

Now and forever I will love,
you are the one my heart dreamed of,
My dream is real.

## _We Call Her Blessed_

In loving memory of my grandmother

I wish that words could plunge the depths
of love within my heart
I'd say the beauty you conveyed
was only just a part
of all you mean to each of us
each day a worry, to fuss a must,
but at the core of who you are,
God's love poured out through you.

A legacy of faith passed down,
wisdom, honor, respect abound,
compassion laced with tenderness,
We rise up and call her blessed.
All along life's narrow way
We can choose to go or continue to stay.
In pride, rejecting Christ's sacrifice
That being good will then suffice.

You found the way to Calvary's cross
You lived each day knowing the cost
To live is vain, to die is gain,
to run the race and ever strain
To win the goal, heaven awaits
And as you walk through pearl studded gates
Jesus awaits with arms open wide
Because you asked Him, "Lord, come inside".

# Petals
# Of
# Friendship

*A friend is someone who will meet you halfway even when the bridge is out.*

-Pam Rowell-Scoggins

# *For David*

Dedicated to David Magowan

My heart is so empty, I have nothing to hold,
Alone and displaced in a prison so cold,
Where were you, my God, when I lost all I love?
The darkness is brutal, I can't feel any touch.
Were you there in the depths when a bomb came to claim
all of my family taken away?
Were you there in the tears as I cried there for days?
Please, tell me where was the strength and the grace?
My heart lay there broken, shattered to bits,
Where were you, God of heaven, answer me this!
They say time is a healer as it ticks now away,
but my pain and my sorrow will not dissipate.
Tell me, my God, where does my hope lie?
I've waited and prayed for an answer on high…
My child, don't you know that I lost all I love?
He was broken and beaten to give grace when times are tough.
He willingly left heaven and came to the earth,
Leaving a throne, a crown – royal birth.
He walked lowly and humble to teach you, my child,
His love is the Way, the Truth and the Life.
He laid down His life, stretched out His arms,
My heart too was broken, completely undone!
For this is your hope in the midst of the dark,
when no light shines about you, not even one spark!
Hold on to Me, My arms reach around
to comfort and keep you, totally sound.
My promise I made to you and I'll keep
Just call on His name in faith now and leap,
He won't disappoint you, never to leave,
For His name is Jesus, my son, to Him cleave!!

# *Friendship's Rose*

To Patricia Hill, on your birthday

The roots of friendship grow so deep
as those of a beautiful red bud rose.
Deep red petals, leaves so green,
intertwined so lavishly.

The sweetness of the Rose is fair
it's scent is carried everywhere,
so is the way with friendship rare,
it bends, it grows, forever there.

Through wind and rain and summer storm,
Friendship's Rose grows unadorned.
Friendship's petals sometimes fall,
but God's the maker of them all.

He designed them just to fit,
together woven bit by bit.
The blood red petals and the thorns
reminders how His love was borne.

Sometimes the way of friendships rough
reach out your hand when things get tough,
look out your window at the Rose
you'll not forget the way of those,

Whose lives were intertwined with yours
two lives directed heavenwards,
to meet again through golden gates,
While on this earth to be soul mates.

# God's Perfect Providence

For Irma Reyes Hatley – God's gift of friendship

Walking in obedience two faithful hearts do beat
in rhythm to God's cadence our paths a narrow street.
The first did move away from home while stepping out in faith.
The second in wilderness to roam wandering in darkest state.
For in God's perfect providence their paths do cross and meet,
in friendship, God shapes confidence
and plants love's tender seed.
I feel unworthy, yet so blessed to know you as my "sister", friend,
but greater still on knees to bend,
we bow our heads to God confess.
With joyful hearts and hands raised high,
to our Lord, we glorify,
we magnify the grace of God
that sent His Son from up above.
You are so mighty, we stand in awe,
Your promises, they have no flaws,
into our lives, Your will to show
and through experience we know.
I am so thankful for this friend,
please show me what Your will is then,
lead us to the perfect place
and make our lives a journey of grace.
When we arrive before Your throne,
please let Your words on us adorn,
"this child held nothing  back from me,
her life was open for all to see".
Then we will fall down on our face,
Your glory bright, our hearts to race,
to place our crowns down at Your feet,
to worship You for all eternity.

# The Class of '85

In memory of Marlene Lucas, Kemp High School

Old photographs of smiling faces
edges torn and frayed
reminders of forgotten places
the memories have stayed.

Some are sweet and some are tragic,
some are dear while others cruel
looking back at times nostalgic
some compare to priceless jewels.

Not all of us through kinship borne
each to his own friends made,
but even now our hearts are torn
thinking back through time now paved.

Sometimes laughter, many tears,
catchy phrases, some were fools,
all were struggling with many fears
wanting acceptance while in school.

Many years have passed us by
what heritage lies within?
Do we inspire a goal to try?
Have our lives a portion to give?

Our lives are fleeting without meaning
our soul's condition doomed to hell,
there is one spark of hope, you see,
Jesus Christ on Calvary's tree.

Don't waste your time on earthly token
there's no reward in gain,
Jesus' words were long ago spoken
to guide our lives in His name.

# Kerry's Song

There is a sad song that he plays in the dark,
it's mournful wail calls and tears at my heart.
His melody is judgment, unforgiveness its strain,
it's Kerry's song and it has no refrain.

He plays it over again to me and thinks that I don't see
the battle he faces, I also face with never a moments reprieve.
For in the dark there is no light, no hope and no peace,
but Jesus hung on Calvary's tree to bring us all of these.

I know your struggle is very real, I feel it in my soul,
but by God's grace and prevailing faith
those "demons" must let go.

Don't think me fragile or made of glass,
my heart is stronger than you know.
My soul in need of comfort, my heart in need of grace,
I am just a woman also struggling in sin's tow.

# Tenderness Came

He reaches out with tenderness,
his eyes shine with years of pain
a sadness, incompleteness on his face have gained,
yet in his soul such sweetness and loving attitude
it touched my heart completely and gave me hope anew.

This tender man the years have torn
and tried it's best to steal,
but he has gained so much more
through Christ, his heart will heal.
What road to choose, what path to take?
Only God in heaven knows.
There is for sure a heart at stake
this choice that you will make.

Is there such a thing as a sweet rose or a southern Belle?
The answer, only your heart knows, I really cannot tell.

A butterfly with once weak wings
with a heart searching for love
one night was touched with simpler things
That flew in just like a dove.

Pure and sweet and gently came
this tenderness from miles away
and now this heart that once was lame
will never be the same.

Fluttering, floating, on the wind,
in flight to where you are,
with open heart, a prayer to send,
until these miles don't seem so far.

# A Man of Honor

In memory of a Ranger

At the time, military life wasn't all it was cracked up to be, and in my mind, I thought I had forever. I wanted to be my own person, experiencing life, testing the proverbial waters as boys do. You were strict and demanding and I was stubborn and stupid not wanting to hear what you had to say.

The harder you pushed, the farther I went, and even though your intelligence took you into dangerous places that your years of training prepared you for, our war was one of the wills and usually yours won out. Even as I rebelled, many things penetrated my thick skull. You passed on a rich heritage to me that I will always cherish.

You birthed confidence in me and moral code and even though you didn't get to see it, my life did turn around. I admire your strength of character and strength of mind, the way you always had the answer even when it was one I didn't want to hear.

I could never live up to your standards, and looking back, I wish I had tried harder. That doesn't mean I didn't love you, because I did, fiercely. I didn't want to voice it out loud, but I hoped to be just a portion of the man you were.

I miss you, Dad. I remember all those times when a simple task became a lesson learned. You were constantly teaching me. I miss those days in the shop, just you and me banging around, being together in comfortable silence. I felt secure and warm.

You were more than just a teacher, you were a mentor. You lived integrity and honesty before me every day. If someone needed you, you were always there. I wish I could have said that I needed you because I needed you more often than I ever said. Thank You, Dad, for passing on so much more than I realized.

Your character was rich and full. I wish for just one more time to tell you how proud I am that you are my Dad. Yes, you were a tough military man, but in my eyes you were always…

My Hero!

## _Man in the Mirror_

As I look in the mirror all that I can see
is a man  beaten down by past mistakes achieved.
As days have turned to years they've taken heavy toll,
until the man I see, is not the man I know.
So many roads to choose this one I know I'd lose
but me, myself and I was the master of my pride.
Lost along the way, loved ones could not stay,
I couldn't hold them then and now I'm lost again.
Imprisoned in my cell, this consequence a hell
to pay for what I've done, a lifetime under the sun.
No, this is what "I" see as your life reflects to me,
A man who needs himself to give the grace that Christ extends.
As I look deep into your eyes, I see many things that I admire.
So many songs to play, so many verses to sing,
so much more joy to bring to those whose lives are hurting,
from a life of isolation, a heart that's torn
and through your music, God can restore
a broken heart, a faith that's lost
a man whose searching, his life the cost,
and through it all, you will see,
you've found yourself, Christ is the key.
I see a man after God's own heart,
his spirit is willing to play the part,
forgive yourself, cast out your doubt
for Jesus' death is what life's about.
So when you look into the glass
don't see yourself as second class.
A sinner?  Yes, but saved by grace,
redeemed by God to run the race.
There will  be hills and deep, deep valleys,
but God has promised, He will not tarry.
He promised to always  be with you
and through His Spirit bring life anew.
So look again into the mirror,

I think you'll see your image clearer,
for when you look, don't see your face,
but looking deeper with eyes of grace,
see Christ in all the things you do
for His light is shining out through you.

# He Rescued Me

For Lynne

The innocence of childhood is such a precious thing,
such beauty in the morning and love to keep you safe.
This should have been my world, no worries to endure,
but at the tender age of five, I was shocked and terrified.
Instead of love and safety, I had to run and hide.
Day after day was beaten, your flesh to glorify.
With screams so often pleading,
with bruises, my heart pleading,
I would crawl back in the dark
and locked away for "safe keeping".

How could this be my world,
as often day by day,
I never knew if I would live,
"someone help me", I would pray.
"I love you, be a good girl", "I'm sorry that I hit you".
Why, oh why this pain,
when all I wanted was to be safe.
Free from hurt, just taken up
into their arms of love,
Until my world turned right side up
instead of black and hateful.

Even in the midst of night, there was a bright and shining light,
Jesus came into my world, His grace and mercy there unfurled.
With tender love, He then reached down
to loose the chains that kept me bound.
He came, resided in my heart and gave me back a missing part. There
was still so much left to endure, but in His presence, I was for sure,
on days of pain, neglect and loss, He was my comfort because the
cross was where His blood poured out for me to atone for sin, to
set me free, to give me life, one day you'll see just how His love has
rescued me!

# The Fragile Seed

For Lynne

Looking back over time
I'm amazed to find
how far our friendship blossomed
how deep our trust has grown.
Though fragile in the beginning
It's woven, wrapped around
until our spirits united
we stand on solid ground.
There were times of sinking sand
and times of wilderness wandering
but through it all Almighty hands
would guide us on to stand.
I never could have dreamed
nor never could have imagined
a friend like you that God ordained
someone I could turn to.
In death's dark night
when surviving, a fight,
to break free from strongholds snare
I always knew how much you cared.
Though thousands of miles separate us,
we're one in Spirit as in Jesus we trust
to make the way as our friendship unfolds
because the seed was planted just as He foretold.
So looking back over time,
I'm amazed to find,
our friendship has grown, our love is strong
and we have weathered fine.

# *Gift of Love*

For Janice Durham

So many times, so many words
describe the way I feel,
it's hard to find the perfect ones
portray the lines for real.

You have been a mentor,
I've even called you "Mom",
your gift of love enclosed the gulf
that's held me, kept me strong.

You always were my teacher,
showing me the way
to faith in God through trials
when I didn't have a song.

I've watched as many loved you
come back to see your face,
and even through the years
your gift is always grace.

And love so pure that reaches out
extending to another,
rich legacy passed down through time
and now it flies asunder,
to land onto new faces
who pass on through your class,
and looking back they'll too discover
nor will their hearts forsake.

# _Oh, Beautiful Rose_

For Monique Renfro

Oh, fragile Rose with weakest stem
at times the light would grow so dim
it seemed as though in storm tossed nights
the wind would rage, no end in sight.
Days and weeks, weeks then years,
the terror grew, the Son drew near,
just as the Light gave life and ray,
the Tempest grew and so enraged.
You thought the end had 'round you come,
nowhere to turn nowhere to run,
but in a place where eye can't see
protective hand placed 'round to keep
you safe from harm, to set you free.
As time was ripe, your petals grew,
the stem had strengthened, time renewed.
The storm that once had threatened you
now to the Son his heart was true.
Oh, Beautiful Rose with grandest stem,
your radiance is my garden's gem
uniquely formed, through wind and rain
My Glory can now radiate!
Don't doubt your place of splendor there,
When I formed you with gentle care,
I placed you in my finest soil,
I knew you'd face so much turmoil.
So now, My Rose, I love you so
rest in this knowledge and as you grow
remember you are a loving creation
My heart swells with pride, pure adulation!

# Unfolding Eternal Love

*Love without THE Bedrock is just a sandy whim of passion, to be blown and tossed by the wind...*
*never to return.*

**-Pam Rowell-Scoggins**

# Prism of Our Love

To Mel on our anniversary

A ripple of reflection caught my eye, a glance
I looked at its depth, got lost in its trance.
A soul broken, battered, abused,
seeking a shelter, spent past used
lost in the choices I stupidly made,
the light caught, then shifted,
the colors then sprayed
into a prism so different, renewed.
As I looked then more deeply,
The colors askew
revealing a bud of love as a man's tenderness
reached out with compassion like soft wings of a dove.
Again the light refracted the color turned red,
as God ordained, directed as to our marriage led.
The prism burst forth gold, as we vowed our lives to each other
and then it lost its luster as the valleys were sown.
A time of great sorrow of loss and deep struggle,
it seemed like the reflection was gone as forever.
The tiniest spark was caught, the light shone again
a light purer, more vibrant as it poured in array
the fire of trials tested over time, burnt out the brine
brought our love to stay.
As I look at the reflection as time has passed us by
My love and deep affection will stay so come what may.
No matter what season
No matter what comes
Our love is the reason
Until life's journey is done.

## *Timeless Love*

To Shawn and Patricia Hill, Happy Anniversary

Candles are lit like shimmering diamonds
luscious red roses scent the air,
all around us gaiety sounds,
but Baby, it's just you and me only here.

My love and my life, I promise once more
never to leave you, only restore.
My heart skips a beat until I can see
your beautiful face always to be
forever with mine side by side.

Our love was ordained,
chosen and placed,
within our hearts from above.
The Father Himself hand-picked both of us
Before there was time, even space.

Our lives now committed,
God, give us all wisdom
as we look at another year past,
we thank you today for this love we've embraced
as we seek to extend to each other.

Help us each day, when it's equally grave
to show grace when our way is so dim,
Your mercy so great
remind us again,
of the cross on that Hallowed hill.

# Two Tender Hearts

To Travis and Tiffany Durham, Jr.


Before the world's foundation
God called, it came to be,
two hearts in preparation
for a lifetime, you and me.
Two tender hearts to meet
distinctly with God's lead
He gave us this true love
that started from above.
This love a divine treasure,
to honor, nurture with pleasure
for when life's trials come,
God holds us through each one.
A love that's woven through
hearts' fibers strong and true
not only with two strands
now three, within God's hands.
We dedicate our lives today
God's plan within His will
and now with greater faith to stand
our hearts to be fulfilled.
Please let our love shine with a light
a beacon burning and so bright
help us not forget the way
a highway sacrifice has paved.
Without the blood of Jesus poured
out for us with so much scorn,
this our hope in marriage lies
with two nail prints and a speared side.
When love feels lost reminisce the cost
to find on Calvary's tree,
for Jesus' love surpassed them
all when He died for you and me.

# *Love Song: The Courtship*

A Trilogy
*Dedicated to my husband, Russell*


He touches me so tenderly
with words so lovely to hear.
My heart responds so deeply,
His voice so smooth and pure,
just like a flower opening to
the light for the first time,
a butterfly breaking free,
spreading her wings to fly.

This so unexpected, yet welcome all the same,
His name calles like a balm, "Beloved", it claims.
A smile on my face, a song in my heart,
music so sweet, soothing and light.
Raindrops dancing, delicate and bright,
pour like a treasure into the night.

His arms fold around me, strong and secure,
they hold me so tight, will never let go.
This love is so beautiful, priceless and rare,
we hold fast together, our love song to share.
We sit so together until the sunrise,
sharing our dreams by the light of the moon.
As the sun comes to greet us, we embrace one more time,
As our lips part, we're breathless,
but we'll be together soon.

# Whispers of Love: The Honeymoon

A trilogy
*Dedicated to my husband, Russell*

As I look at your face, my eyes meet your eyes
so deeply, I see, you've fallen for me.
We reach out to touch so tentatively
so reverent for you, so sweetly for me.

Our whispers of love we share in the night
yearning and craving to be satisfied.
Loving and holding, intertwined by moonlight,
it pours over us with contentments deep sigh.

I give all I have completely to you,
no reservations, wholly assured.
My heart and my soul, you stole long ago
my body is yours on this night to hold.

Our love is eternal, forever to share,
tonight all is perfect, we have not a care,
the glow of our love, it shines with a light
illuminating our path that we walk in the night.

Please hold me, My Love, don't ever let go,
when darkness descends, we'll look up above
and find once again our love in the night,
where passions strong fire will burn again bright.

# Love's Lasting Promise: Growing Old Together

A trilogy
- *Dedicated to my husband, Russell*

As the years pass us by, our love still takes flight
on wings of a prayer with heaven in sight.
Our love is a rhythm, a song all our own,
it's steady pulse plays in our hearts there so strong.
it's more than a dance, a rhyme or a beat,
it's more than just passion on fire or heat.
It makes our breath catch when we look at each other,
it's like a well that reaches down further.
It makes the sky blue and gives color hue,
it's tender and sweet yet held so together
by love's lasting promise that says it's forever.

Through time tortured moments, we've been far apart,
and then so close together to hear each other's heart.
Through struggle and rain, sometimes even pain,
our love has stood strong even through seasons of change.
So reach out your hand, as we walk side by side,
when fear grips your heart, take comfort and hide
hold onto me, my loves a safe place,
my arms always open ready for your embrace.
Through stormy seas and times of great joy
this music, our song, will leads us back home.

Where you'll always find my heart waiting for you
to love you and keep you and know I'll be true.
We may have grown old, but our love's fresh and new.
You light up my world that each day sees me through.
For all of eternity, I would never grow tired
of saying "I love you" because you inspire
so many good things as the years have gone by
I cherish you more – your love's the reason why!

# The Promise

To Jeff and Chasity Thompson

Her Beloved

The day is dawning  bright and clear
The birds are singing sweet love song
Each arrives with vision pure
A promise made from heav'n above.
Today, I'll take your hand in mine
No more doubt or hint of fear.
I will take you as my wife
We'll vow our love, the world to hear.

The Beloved

The Revelation's been made clear
The appointed time has come
Long and hard, the journey here,
Until through God, I found the one.
Many roads, I've traveled down,
I look in awe as we stand here.
We dedicate our lives to Him,
I'm ready to become your wife.

Refrain:

Finally, I take your hand
We bow down before the Son,
We vow our lives to share
Nevermore to be apart.
It's ingrained onto our hearts
Just like you promised from the start

# The Blessing

The heavens burst with a light
That shines down on us tonight.
The promise made so long ago
Is now complete, it is done
Just the way you sent your Son
Your mercy's more than we deserve.
As we walk in this new life
Help us keep you when the night
Tries to darken and blot out the Son.
And as days turn to years,
We'll look back and know for sure
This is the path you planned all along.
So thank you Father, for the Son,
Thank you, Jesus for your blood,
Thank you Father, for loving us so much!
We thank you Father for loving us so much!

# These Words

*To my husband, Russell*

I could write the words for love
and never quite convey
the feelings in my soul for you
as they have given way.
Rich words like beautiful, priceless, rare,
for these are who you are,
and others still like
soft, beloved, charming, cherished
for these are in my heart.
How can I possibly tell you
all the words I have for you?
For they consume and gently call
like a sweet, fresh morning dew.
They fall on me, and wrap me up in sweet desire so new.
Just when I think I've said them all more pour out for you.
Words like honor, treasure, shield,
and then my heart just stops
because there's more like passion, deep desire and want.
A fierce flame burns, so strong, intense,
and then my heart just leaps
for right beside that there is more
like righteousness and peace.
I've never felt such deep fulfillment
never a love so complete,
But you, My Love, have captured me,
And now you have my heart!

Fallen
Petals
Of
Sorrow

*Sorrow lasts for the longest season, but joy will break through and*
*bring a brighter day...*
*just over the horizon.*

-Pam Rowell-Scoggins

# *Where's the Music?*

Someone unplugged my heart today,
amidst the roses and the music
a thief came and stole my very center
and now the pieces don't all fit
I shove them left and throw them right
no matter what, there's still no clue
I beat my breast and cut myself
I only see the blood.

There is no meaning without the heartbeat
and that was taken away.
I can't hear the music, yet I feel it's beat.
The rhythm beats with the noise but I can't find the music
Where's the music?

The melody was stripped from the song
and now there is no harmony.
Amidst the roses there are thorns
and one is lodged in me.
It pierced me through and through and now the pain gives way to
ebb and flow and mingled blood as now the music fades and all that's
left of the once sweet music are the cries and moans of my soul,
lost without the melody,
as the blood drains away
and my soul turns to dust
blowing across the desert rose.

# _Gone_

Love wrapped around my heart,
joy overflowed this rim,
happiness could not describe
this heart that love shone within.
I loved you more than breath or life –
Angels kissed the dew,
because the world was new –
Where once was I,
now there's only you –
There is no greater love
a winged prayer
from heaven's lips
fell on me and then made you.
The day drew near,
I'd see your form,
to look and find you there,
"So sorry ma'am, no life is here,
it's been lost somehow, I don't know…"
My mind went numb,
all thoughts were stripped away.
Goodness, light and life were aborted that day.
These legs, they walk, this voice, it speaks,
My heart, it beats,
but living is just existing because
my baby's gone and left me here.

# _Crushed_

Confusion all around me,
I grasp at endless straws,
the thread of hope now out of reach
as the endless pit snatches it away.

I push down panic,
after all, God is a miracle worker,
surely He isn't cruel
and would not crush me with His foot.

As panic gives way to the deepest sorrow –
Only Mothers know this love
that so engulfs you, so takes you
that it no longer can be defined, it's so far reaching.

It can't be spoken or words
do justice to its form,
only the heart knows and mine was touched
and now it is crushed.

Confusion all around me
I lay dazed and stripped bare
for where once there was a miracle,
is now a nightmare.

# *Forgotten Lullaby*

Silently, she sits rocking
Silently, she strokes the air
Silently, she sings the tune
Forgotten lullaby.

The day rushes by
but dull eyes don't see
don't take in the world
just silent gaze, staring.

She rocks,
She strokes,
She sings,
Silently mourning
while life rushes by.

The lullaby of tender pink skin,
so soft and sweet,
The lullaby goes 'round in her head.

Silently stroking the air,
Silently dying inside,
Silently singing as

The lullaby is forgotten on the wind.

## The Long Night of My Soul

The endless black corridor
the slinking away of the dense fog
thick and sticky as heat
stretches across your skin.

Fear that claws at your throat and strangles your breath
releasing it right before the blackness claims you.
A bony hand that thrusts around your beating heart,
squeezing the life out of it.

This is the long night of my soul.
The nights when the pain shreds
my heart over and over
until all that's left are pieces
that will never fit together again.

Long night of my soul,
please release me from my agony,
if you would only leave my dying heart alone.
You've stripped my womb,
torn out my heart,
and crushed my soul,

When, oh night, will you dry my tears,
cease my silent moans
and bring life to me again?
When will the long night be over??

## _Would You_

Would you have been a boy or a girl?
Would you have been short or tall?

Would you have had blue eyes or green, maybe brown?
Would you have had dotted cheeks like your Daddy's
or would you have had my smile?
I wonder all these things as I think of you, my child.

You never got to grow
and never could you know
the wonders and beauty of this life.

Would you have been a doctor
or a teacher or even a missionary?
Would you have done great things to be recognized for
or would your life have been uneventful here
while laying treasure up above?

I'll never know while on this earth
but maybe up in heaven,
God will see fit to show me why
My Angel had to be taken?

## *No Moments*

I know it seems selfish on a day when great men and women are
remembered for their sacrifices in battle that all I can think about
is that you're not growing in my tummy. I'll never know your flut-
tering, I'll never feel your kick. I found such joy in every part even
when I was sick. I'll never have the pain required to bring you into
this world. I'll never have that first moment when your beautiful cry
rings out, I'll never count your fingers and toes and make sure that
they all fit.
I'll never snuggle you at my breast and have that bond so strong, I'll
never hear your first word,
would it be "Mommy or Da-Da"?
Whichever would be good. There'll be no moments of tucking you
into bed and reading you a story.
No moments when you stay out late and I begin to worry.
I'll never know your achievements and failures
the times when I stand proud,
and times to scream and cheer for you out loud.
There will be no moments of kissing the hurt away,
of taking you in my arms and making it okay.
There'll be no years of growing up and having decisions to make or
summer comes and when at last it's time to take a break. You'll have
no graduation moments, no wedding and no love – that was stripped
away one spring as from above,
God took you back to live with Him,
I got no say at all
and now I'm left with pain and grief
and there's no sense at all!

# Life Moves On

Heart, broken heart,
You shattered into a million miniscule pieces
and there is no miracle for you here.

Heart, shattered heart,
Just lie there until the life blood drains away
There is no transfusion just the ceaseless bleeding.

Heart, bleeding heart,
Slowly dying, there's nothing left to help you
and the darkness is rushing up to claim you.

Heart, dying heart,
Wasn't it just yesterday when life was utopia
and nine months away would be paradise?

In the blink of an eye,
all that's good,
all that's sacred simply vanishes
with the wad down the toilet.

Heart, lifeless heart,
So still and cold in my breast,
I'm chilled and pale and now life moves on –
trampling the cold, dead form of who I use to be,
but will never be again.

# *Baby Doll*

She made her list and checked it twice –
At the top –
BABY DOLL –
One who eats and wears a diaper.
Her nine year old heart bulging with love for her new "baby".
Every year, her wish list included a BABY DOLL
and every year until she was twelve,
she cherished that little plastic body
and immovable blinking eyes –
She finally outgrew baby dolls, but her mothering, maternal nature
longed for the day when she would hold her own baby.
Married at 21, her dreams in her eyes, but no baby came and divorce
claimed her, shattering her again.
She vowed to remain single –
but as God would have it, her soul mate, the one meant for her,
claimed her heart once more.
She dared to hope, hoped to dream as years would pass away that one
day when lovers rule, her dream would come to stay?
Excitement, love, abandon claimed her heart that day,
but as we live and breathe,
the darkness did it's part –
It stripped her womb, crushed her heart –
It stole more than just a life –
It took her spirit and her dreams –
Hope died and tore her apart.

# Beyond Myself

You are gone now as I start my day
and I remember the way you look at me,
the way you see me.

The way you love me and touch me
and I know that you are in my heart
as I go about my day.

I will carry this special memory with me
as I hurdle the mountain and struggle out of the valley,
as life trips me
and when I fall.

I'll stretch myself to go beyond myself,
to reach out to the unknown and show who I am
deep in my soul.

Because you are the one constant in my life
and without you,
I am just wandering
blowing in the wind.

# Shades
# Of
# Color

*Looking through a prism, different hues appear, shades of color never seen, revealed become so real.*

- Pam Rowell-Scoggins

# _A Christmas to Remember_

The Christmas tree was decorated with pretty red bows,
and old-fashioned balls that twinkled like gold.
Little white lights shone mixed intertwined,
they winked and they blinked as each branch there was lined.
Candy canes so cute, they hung here and there and icicle strands to
give the tree the yuletide glow.
Picture pretty packages placed 'round the tree,
they were all wrapped up for little girl eyes to see.
Tall ones, small ones with big round red bows,
long ones, short ones even mistletoe.
It seemed all was perfect on this Christmas night,
as each gift was opened with wonder and might.
Yet in her little girl heart there was still something missing,
a place way down deep that was endless and empty.
That night as she bowed on her knees beside her bed,
she began, "Dear Father", her sweet little girl prayer,
"I thank you for all the wonderful things that Mommy and Daddy
and Santa could bring",
but then with a pause and a catch in her voice,
she said, "oh, but Jesus, He's the best gift by choice,
to bring to the world all of the things,
we miss and we need on this Christmas Eve.
So thank you, my Father, for the best gift indeed,
Jesus, My Savior, and He's there just for free!"
As she bound into bed and snuggled into her sheets,
Mommy and Daddy tucked her in with tears on their cheeks.
No worry in their hearts for this little one
for this moment in time would stand still as time ticked on.
For this was truly a Christmas to remember,
as their little girl and her sweet gentle prayer,
made Jesus her choice on this day to remember
that He is our hope and not just in December!

# The Story of Old

The night calm and silent, the wind so still
all the earth hushed as if each creature could feel,
the birth pangs of heaven, the story of old,
the stable, the manger, for generations was told.
The Savior would be born and laid down so lowly,
Jesus, the Christ-child, so humble and holy.
Angels bathed in the pure glorious light
the shepherds were watching their flocks that night,
so unaware of the miracle they would know
for this was the night prophets foretold.
Quaking and trembling, shrinking with fear,
their eyes unbelieving as the message to hear,
"Behold, good news I bring to you,
great joy that is true,
He comes for all the people
He is salvation for all of you."
Just then the heavens filled, the night sky burst forth,
thousands of angels announcing Jesus' birth,
praising God in the highest and proclaiming peace on earth
to every man who pleases God as through their lives to trod.
The miracle of Christmas was born that blessed night
He was wrapped in swaddling clothes snuggled up tight
shepherds were told as angels announced,
"Behold I bring you good tidings of great joy
today in Bethlehem a Savior is born!"
Just as the shepherds on that 1st Christmas night were part of the
wonder as the north star shone bright and just as they worshipped the
Christ-child that day let our hearts rejoice with the gift that same way,
and shine forth the hope as we wait for His return,
that others will know Him
and have eternal life for certain.

# My Christmas Wish

My wish for you on this Christmas Eve
is that your heart will be hopeful
and filled with belief,
that just as the Christ-child was born so long ago,
and laid in a manger and told as of old,
and just as He came, the perfect Lamb of God,
to go to the cross and bear each one's shame,
to die in your place and take on your sin
and then on the third day be raised to life again.

This gift not under a tree,
It cannot be found, nor human eye see
It cannot be bought or earned in degree
This gift is just that:    a gift of belief.

So remember in this season of gifts and receiving,
the only gift worth giving is the child of lowly birth.
This is the gift not wrapped under the tree
but in this Christmas season, it's a gift of hope, joy and peace,
let's celebrate everyday and let others see
the Royal King Jesus in splendorous array,
won't you give others this gift of salvation today?

For yesterday is gone and tomorrow's unsure,
Why not today to give a soul's sin-sick cure?
And unveiling the Savior for blind eyes to see
to reach out with hope to someone downcast
to lift up the down trodden and share Jesus at last!

So on the Eve of Emmanuel's day,
all that I hope for and all that I pray
is that Jesus resides in each of your hearts
and you'll take Christmas with you
each day make it a part!

# A Tribal Fire

A deep dark forest rain
a steady rhythm played,
bare feet all dance around,
a tribal fire mound.

Painted faces, voices chanting
arms are raised with bodies slanting
bending, reaching toward the sky
with lifted heads and hands held high.

A song of celebration for
a baby born as feelings soar
old traditions now passed down
keeping rhyme to drums that sound.

A torch is lit to signal life
a great occasion to pass the pipe
a circle represents the past
a history meant to last.

His name will bear the mark of one
who he is, what he'll become
his roots run down a river deep
while expectations, they are steep.

For this moment time stands still
this life has all their dreams fulfilled
for when this son has grown to find
he'll be the leader next in line.

# _Paradise is Real_

Paradise is real –
I will live there –
there are sinners –
saved from sin –
because they'll know no hell –
it is apart from God.

"Eden" was a place
where perfection dwelt
there was no thirst or hunger
because God daily kept.

Yes, there is a God, my Father
who dwells up in the sky
He knows my very being
and the place and time I'll die
no need to walk the "Jasper barefoot"
golden streets for me to see?
I need not long for Eden
heaven's gates are certainty!

# *Emerald City*

There is an emerald city
my eyes have never seen
It's beauty it surpasses
any image my mind conceives.
The ocean holds its borders,
rocky crags jut out so steep,
the land is lush and velvet
with a carpet of grass so green.
The splendor of its mountains reach
to the heavens cast overhead,
a pot of gold, a rainbow
arches down in valleys meet.
My heritage, its roots start there in lilting Irish tongue,
Ancestry born so long ago before Christendom.
I long to see its richness and hear its wailing song,
I want to trudge its valleys
and stand in spiral sun.
I'm longing to discover
my place in its history,
I'm willing to uncover
these things my eyes will see.
For there within its mass is the mystery of my past,
and so much in the future that will change my life at last!
So this is the beginning
of dreams I've wished to come true
and finally I will know
what my heart already knew.

# The Old Oak Tree

The old oak tree stood,
a silent statue of long forgotten laughter
and dark times of pain.
The gray lines painted his weathered face
and branches drooped, slightly bent with age.

His roots reached down deep cavities in the earth,
strengthening his trunk
through storm-tossed skies and gale force winds.
His stately stature looked down on his kingdom,
his breadth of branches bringing forth protection to his clan.

All the while, his proud presence seemingly unnoticed
as the generations marched by.

# *February*


February –
Its breath silently dances around
the last hope of January's frost nippin' at your nose,
icicles hang like frozen tombs
against the white washed sky,
ushering in the gale of March winds
and torrential rain.
A time for lovers
and the tender blooms of spring
invite anticipation of things to come.
The old leaves stripped away
and bare branches reach up
beckoning a fresh coverlet.
The world holds its breath
as the glacial grip of February
releases its hold
one icy finger at a time
to give birth to new life.

# My Reality Check

Have you had a reality check lately?
Well, I have one every time I look in the mirror.
I find new lines on my face and around my eyes,
New aches and pains that seem to have formed overnight
and new gray hair that just sticks out when my color starts to fade.
Forget 40, when I became 35, I  felt like I was sliding down the pro-
verbial hill and hit every stump and rock on my spiral down.  How is
it that you can go to bed feeling perfectly okay at 34,
and wake up at 35 feeling like a Mack truck just ran over you?
I will never know on this earth, but one day I will be perfect
when I die and go home to be with my Savior.
Until then, Aleve and Tylenol are my two best friends,
Sports Crème and Clairol make me feel like a new woman,
And NO ONE can tell me it's downhill from here because
I've already hit the bottom of the hill with a resounding THUD!

# *Winter*


It hangs like the stench of death in the air
nothing moves, nothing breaths, all life is sucked out
as the jutting of scarecrow branches
reaches out to snatch what's left.

Perception turns to mindless mush
trampled in afterthoughts of light and life
that get lost somewhere
between yesterday and tomorrow.

Suspended,
packed into frozen graves
while timeless, forgotten limbs
sway and moan with the weight of too much burden.

# *America Will Rise*

*IN MEMORY AND TRIBUTE TO THOSE LOST IN THE ATTACK
ON AMERICA, SEPTEMBER 11TH*

In the midst of the darkness, rising in pride
from destruction and rubble, determined, head high,
America will rise though many have fallen
courageous men and women their lives not forgotten.
Heroes among us in flight and on land,
restoring our trust 'til united we stand.
Hands across America, the Land of the Free,
looking toward purple mountains majesty.
"Old Glory" stands tall, she will not give way
to cowards in ignorance whose actions did sway
these deeds of darkness, hatred and pain,
for where there is senseless death there can be no gain.
We honor your memory, in tribute we stand,
we lovingly salute you with torn hearts and helping hands.
Ingrained in our minds this horrific terror,
when under attack, our nation comes together.
We won't sit by in silence or cower in fear,
but now in the darkness, our vision is clear.
Swift judgment and wisdom, a long arm indeed,
this act on our land brings justice with speed.
In history past, our enemies have tried
to hurt us, defeat us, but in courage and pride,
we've shown all the world what America's made of.
Freedom, independence, unity and strength,
equality for all with opportunities to seek
September 11th a dark day, we think,
America will rise, a united nation, indeed!!!

# Hollow of the Night

In the hollow of my bones, further than the marrow,
past tangible and before obsolete,
dwells an ache that latches onto the sinews and tendons
with needle-like fingers sending spasms down the highway of nerves
colliding with all sensibility and norm.
All thought of what was known is no more.
Like an intruder, my world is stolen and insufferable.
Nothing fits into the lines and curves
but rushes sideways, up and down, away…
Futile are my graspings, senseless are my moans,
just as I reach the light, I'm thrust back down again.
Clenching, clutching, clawing until flesh gives way.
The bone-chilling stillness of night clutches my very life source
strangling all hope and as I gasp one last time,
I cry out to the light to save me…

Then the light breaks across the dawn illuminating the night…

Whisperings of yesterday,
happen chance applauds,
reaching past old hurts
to see what lies beyond,

through long dark night
and cold cement grave,
to finally grasp the key,
the floods of time unlock my memory.

As the pain rushes up to crush me,
the Light pours over and holds me
warmth enfolds my fragility
and I leave the door open.

# *Untitled*

Why do you tread so softly,
when all within you rages?
Do you think that walking quietly
will help you through the stages
of grief and bitter envy as the days roll on?
Do you comprehend the ending to the song,
or are you content to play the never ending beginning
as it drones on and on?

To lash out would be such relief
instead of faking a deep belief
in something you can't understand
and even if you did, what would be the point?
Be real, just feel the gut wrenching pain.
Express the moans in your soul
don't go insane
from trying to save face and act so cool
when putting up a front only makes you a fool.

So when life throws a knife and strikes you down
don't put a band aid on the gushing blood
call down your healing from up above
and search the One who knows you best
He will never leave you nor forsake
your battered heart, and desperate state
with tender hands, He'll hold your heart
and stop the bleeding and stitch it up
and when the pain begins to fade
You can trust Him to keep you safe.

# A Lesson Learned

What life lies in this cold, dark night?
Is it to find a blanket warm?
Where does the wind seek comfort when
it's always tattered and torn?
And when the stars frolic in distant sky,
who shoots the moon for them?
If they tire of lighting up the night,
what happens when they dim?

What of the sun in scorching heat,
who cools his tongue in sweet relief?
And when the days drag on so long
who holds his hand and says, "come along!"
And when the moon lights up the night,
who takes his place if he leaves too soon?

Just as the night is cold and dark
and as the wind just takes to flight
the dancing stars and round full moon
lend light unto those travelers few
that find the narrow path that leads
down to the valley, up mountains steep
and stops before the Great White Throne
it was His voice they listened for.

He told the night so sleepy, full
and told the wind when not to stall,
each star was placed so perfect fit
to lend the night, each one was lit
and sun so warm up in the sky
gives life and light to passersby
and so each one content to be
within the Masters plan so free

to act and do as each was made
and never would they voice complaint.
So in this lesson we can see
to live as He created you to be!

## The Path to Freedom

The wailing sea of deep blue green
the frothy ocean tide
crashed down upon the age old rocks
with lines of deepened pride.
Generations stood on this scenic hill
gazed to starry skies
and dreamed the dream of every heart
for that wherein each lies.

To sail across the deepest sea
or on this lush land stand?
To forge a new existence
or stay on sacred ground?
Is this the trail to freedom or is it yonder there?
For some it was, others never knew
and those who came weren't sure.

They came not knowing what they'd find
distant shores they beckoned, called,
they left all that they knew behind
a voyage to the unknown.
The path to freedom might have been found
but piercing deeper still
to the soul, not hindered, not bound,
the key to freedom's trail.

## Sonnet I

O Love, what mysteries lie in thy sight?
For loves' fair maiden in minds eye must be,
milk-creamy skin like soft silk to touch thee,
twin stars, I see to gaze in wintry night,
like sweet song that lilts on fresh mornings flight,
deep longing swells within my soul to keep
a stirring fire that in my breast does leap,
that locks my heart entombed in sin-sick plight!
O Love, release thy grip you have on me!
To taste a kiss so deep within my mind
and then a craving claws released to see
your lovely face is blurred when love is blind,
I ask again, O Love, sweet misery!

## Sonnet II

Alas! My love sick heart does crave to see
the moonbeams shining down cast you in light
as beauty mingles with the dark of night
loves sweet rapture is perfect as can be,
the winds serenade plays a harmony.
As I awake from sleep my heart enslaved
startled to find again my Love has flown
to a place where dreams are wild and free
I search the night where has my true love gone?
Was his kiss a cruel attempt to put aright
those things my heart cries out to be fulfilled?
No hint or trace I find as morning dawns.
Did I hallucinate my dream to life?
Alas! I close my eyes to lay there still.

*Unopened Packages Of Hope*

*Hope is birthed through the trials and blossoms in the rose garden.*
*Watch them as they unfold..*

*in the glory of His Light.*

-Pam Rowell-Scoggins

# By Grace Restored

Broken shards of glass are laid
her heart a shattered key
her life in ruins, wracked with pain
she longs to just be free.

Her concentration camp is walled
with bitterness and rage
unforgiveness loudly calls
"look around, this is my stage."

Her rooms of life are etched with hate
from some atrocity
her childlike innocence the fate
of man's monstrosity.

With agony, her soul does ache
the memories she longs to raze
her suffering robbed what use to be
long, sunny days carefree.

Forced to walk from room to room
no trophies and no pride
with little left that's not consumed
there's no where she can hide.

And then one day with shocked surprise
a knock rings out, her heart has cried,
"It's him!  It's him! He's at the door,
there is no mercy ever more."

Her heart is fragile, her strength is frail,
with trembling hand, and face gone pale,
she reaches out to grasp the door
not knowing what's in store.

A prayer so silent on her breath
with courage in the face of death
unlocking, turning, grasping for
that heavy prison door.

For just a moment, gripped with fear,
her vision blurred and not so clear,
for shining light deeply it pours
where once was dark interior.

Looking down, a box she found
she opened it to see,
gently, tenderly unbound
restored, lay her hearts key.

Then she fell onto her knees
the ground to meet her face,
for years gone by with silent plea
she found her gift of grace.

Beloved, are you crushed with care?
Your soul in need of prayer?
A gift awaits at your hearts door
please open up, let grace restore.

With love, this gift stretched out his arms
was nailed up on a tree,
His hands reached out to take the scars
His resurrection power free.

This gifted box each one awaits
Jesus' mercy a price so great
outside your prison door the key,
to grace, He gave you bountifully.

# Seeds of Hope

Her eyes are deep blue ocean depths
with specks of darkened green,
Her face is light tan from the sun
Her hands are worn and stained.

Her hair dark brown and flowing from
a crown, so thick a mane,
her arms are strong with legs so tall
they reach across the plain.

Get lost in ocean depths of blue
the windows to her soul, it's true
with jagged scars embedded there
her song she cannot share.

It speaks of love and painful loss
failed ways in life she tried.
She never counted all the cost
for she has never cried.

She paints her smile upon her face
she closes her hearts door.
The pain and loss are neatly tucked
to remember nevermore.

She is not yet a woman
just merely a child
her few short years while on this earth
have robbed her meek and mild.

As innocence is lost, not found
look deep into her depths
the stories hidden, stored and bound
so neatly they are kept.

No worth she feels in life at all
these walls hold her confined
until her heart, it opens up
on which some seeds can fall.

So judge her not by what you see
her life will not be wasted
Jesus died for you and me
God's grace a great oasis.

With hand stretched out, He took the nail
for she was on His mind
when seeds of hope are sown in hearts,
His touch will never fail.

Seeds spring to life to grow inside
each heart by love refined,
for if it weren't for Jesus Christ
our lives no more a prize.

# The Runner

Dedicated to Jim and Polly Feemster
In Memory of Jim

A runner poised with strength and grace,
he must keep up a steady pace,
down deep, dark valleys, up mountaintops,
this race to win and never stop.

Small victories along the way,
when battles come, He will not sway,
but keep his focus on the Son,
for in His name the race begun.

Life's hurdles try to beat him down
to make him quit and keep him bound,
this runner by the grace of God,
keeps in God's presence, feet pounding sod.

Through many trials with tested faith,
this runner holds to God's mercy and grace,
because he sees the perfect prize,
eternity at Jesus' side.

He could take the easy path,
for in his sin, he deserved God's wrath,
in God's great love, He made provision,
His eyes are fixed with clearest vision.

For in mind's eye, an old rugged tree,
hung Jesus nailed for all to see,
His love for us was there outpoured
with His blood, His body, broken, torn.

The runner sees this love divine
we are but branches, God is the vine
so, he will run to win the race,
receive a crown at Jesus' feet to place.

# *Pressing On*

In Memory of Donald Thompson
Philippians 3:12-14


I am not perfect as you can see
but I press on as Jesus took hold of for me,
continually straining toward the goal
forgetting the past, the future to take hold.

His glory and majesty in my mind's eye
pulls me forward to keep pressing on
knowing one day that prize waits for me
when I get to heaven, my Jesus, I'll see.

And if by some chance, a crown I'll receive,
there's only One who took all my scorn
and He's the only One I'll bow down for
I'll place my crown at His feet for Him to adorn.

I'll walk by His side until that day
Remembering His scars as He made the way.
My privilege is to be like Him in death
to be raised in His likeness, never missing a step.

So I'll keep pressing on knowing one day,
that my life will at once fade fast away
but my hope is Jesus as my Spirit takes flight
and rests in the knowledge: my faith will be sight!

# Heaven's Blessings

Dedicated to Mr. and Mrs. L. E. Bechtol
In Memory of Oma Jean


Blessings fall from heaven
at times we don't know why,
sometimes they come forever
at times just for awhile.

Our lives are unsuspecting
from God's hand which is protecting
from the heart of God sent down
on cherub's wings of prayer.

A gift, these precious blessings,
take care to hold them dear,
and when our path leads separate ways
they'll stay forever near.

Blessings fall from heaven
to touch and change our lives,
they rest within our hearts intent
and will rejoice to meet again!

# My Tears Were in the Rain

Inspired through a conversation with Irma Reyes Hatley

My Child, I called for you
with loving and tender sound
you ran around so quickly
stressed out, so deeply bound.

As clouds around me gathered,
I felt so immensely pained,
I long to tell you great things,
My tears were in the rain.

I watched you as you struggled,
in your own strength to overcome,
but fiery darts had landed,
I knew the deed was done.

My heart was gravely pierced
as my name you spoke in vain,
the rift so small it started,
now a chasm of sin inlaid.

I watched you as you fell,
I wept as you turned away
My heart completely  broken
as you went about your day.

No time to stop and talk
to the Creator of the Universe,
no time to be empowered,
no time for kingdom first.

We labor all the while,
what do we have to gain?
when Jesus Christ is second?
Our lives we live in vain.

We wonder why things go so bad
when we rush around,
we leave in haste, begin our day
forget the TRUTH, the WAY!

Our Prince of Peace awaits our call
He'll never force our will
He's standing by so patiently
our hearts desire to fill.

Why do we linger in our sin
and take the broadest path?
The Lord of lords and King of kings
waits with bated breath.

We miss our blessings every day
when we fail to pray,
abundant life is so much more
than material things that sway.

My child, please take my nail-scarred hand
so lovingly reached out
for in that moment, when I was pierced,
your name, I thought about.

With searing pain and blood stained face,
I made your sins my own,
I could have come down from the cross,
redemption never atoned.

I chose to stay, loved filled my heart,
I long so for that day

to see your face and hold you close,
nevermore, My child, to stray.

So child, please know how much I care
I hurt when you're too busy,
to take the time to bow your knee
and talk with Me in prayer.

# The Gift

Amid the chaos and heartbreak of life
just outside my window,
I wander through the white powdery paths
that lead to my salvation.

My feet take me where
my musings cannot go.
As I gaze heavenward,
my spirit seeks the only comfort, the only solace.

Branches reach up
with white arms and spindly fingers
looking for answers that don't seem to come.

My wanderings take me deeper into a place
that engulfs me
and my heart is overwhelmed
as I see the beauty in death
stretch across everything
it's like the heavens open up
and as a new dusting begins to fall,
this is the response from heaven:

Sometimes you can't understand why –
even if I told you, you wouldn't comprehend,
but My child, know that this gift is from Me
and I made this place and time
just for you to see…

# _So Long the Road_

Sometimes the road we're traveling down
is paved with rocks and looks unsound,
but as it twists and turns and crooks
the God of Truth whose feet once took
the very lane, His pierced feet
as all along the path you meet

His steps so clear, to guide you near
just stay the path and you will hear
His still small voice, the rushing wind
keep walking toward, around the bend,
then day meets day, and night descends
the road outstretched and never ends.

Until the day, as feet wing flight
and leave the earth and meet the Light
while breaking through the plane below
your eyes will open, you will know,
the road that seemed so long with loss
it was the one that lead from the cross
as He outstretched His nail pierced hand
He took the blow, the pain to stand
and at the end of that long road
He stands, He waits, it's paved with gold.

# Your Promised Child

For Tonya

Your hand reached down
and from shapeless form,
You molded, You made me
the breathe of life borne
into her womb, perfect and priceless
Your greatest gift, no flaw just preciseness.

A mother to be through torturous times
sleepless nights, and great yearnings,
tossing and turning,
molding, creating, breathing new life
for a baby so perfectly sound.

Impatience and heartache
through years of much pain,
sadness and sorrow to my heart were chained,
not slow to act, your promise you gave
unveiled in the flesh of this precious babe.

Forgive me, O Lord, for doubting unfair
Your preparation for this great affair.
Your timing is perfect,
Your love, a jewel rare,
You blessed me so much, how can I despair?

Your love for me shown
in this package, I know
Your will and desire
have equally grown
in this promise with little pink toes.

# *Pure Devotion*

For Ryan and Danielle Lintleman


With hearts of pure devotion
led by the Spirit of God,
you came with sweet emotion
a love by example led.
As time would pass and you would grow
a branch that lasts your fruit would show.

As God would pave the way in you
you'd lead and stay forever true.

And now, the path will separate
still keeping on the narrow way
as footprints that at first unseen
forever etched in memory.

They lead us to the cross of Christ
The Lamb of God is glorified
in humble adoration
You took the cross upon yourself.

Just as you've walked the narrow way
and kept your hearts so pure
rest in the fact that God's ways are best
I'm blessed to have known you!

# The Lamb of Glory

A crown of thorns,
a royal robe
his hands were torn,
they hailed Him, "Lord!"
He was beaten and bruised,
a donkey He rode
the cattails abused,
they bowed and adored.
Led up a hill,
palm branches spread
loud thunder pealed,
"Hosanna!" they sang.
As the sky turned black,
a following He gained.
The Father turned His back,
the people's refrain:
They cried out, "Crucify!"
as the Son said, "It is finished",
He was led like a Lamb,
to give His life away.
That's not the end,
the third day it came,
God's power was sent,
as the stone rolled away!
"Jesus is risen!" the power of death broken,
raised and alive, Jesus sits enthroned,
His glory a light as His name is made known.
Glory to God,
Hallelujah to the Lamb!
He is perfect and pure the Lamb that was slain.
Lift up your hands
raise a banner to His name
The King of kings is now the Lamb of Glory!
Let our praise so exclaim!

## Hope Pours Down

Hope pours down afresh and anew
as tears bathe the earth from heaven's buckets of dew.
It washes our eyes with the gentle downpour,
which makes us see what life has in store,
soaking the good as the bad courses down
and falls as the mud puddles pool on the ground.

As the downpour slows to delicate rain drops
the plump, lazy sun peeks out from the clouds
no longer constrained by my circumstance
I cling to the Rock as my hope soars again.

Settling at once my worn-weary heart
plucking the strings as I open it up,
to receive the stinging spray as the once dreary day
flips up my frown as the light then surrounds
all of my problems I thought were so bad.

# Mercy's Love

For Becky Murdock


In the choking darkness, your life line lifts me out
Your mercy, I'm unworthy and my life of no account.
Even as my world tilts down, Your unfailing love will keep me sound
and as my heart rejoices,
I hear the heavens sing:

"My mercy came pouring down from a tree that day.
My Son, I placed against that rough and rugged tree to pay
for all your sin and shame, He is the Truth, He is the Way,
and mercy's love held back the cry
of a thousand angels that day."

He is holy, He is holy, God Almighty, Lord, Jehovah,
Lamb of Mercy, My Shield and Fortress,
The Rock I stand on, the only Way!

"My mercy came pouring down from a tree that day.
My Son, I placed against that rough and rugged tree to pay
for all your sin and shame, He is the Truth, He is the Way,
and mercy's love held back the cry
of a thousand angels that day."

# Your Tender Mercies

For Nancy King

Softly the wind blows, through the night
billowing in and out of my life,
the dark sounds around me, nothing to see
sighing and swaying, my soul in deep need.

A spirit in darkness, clinging to life
with the dawn of a new day, Your mercies in flight,
going before me, preparing the way
planting the seed of hope in grief's wake.

I rest in Your comfort, I'm not all alone,
before there was time, before I was known,
You looked down the road to this appointed time
and proportioned Your love so here I would find,

Someone to hold me, someone to grieve,
Someone to love and be a friend in my need,
Someone to pray, to show me they care,
Someone to unburden my heart to and share,

I feel so unworthy of these blessings so great,
I know that Your timing has never been late.
Just for this season, and just for this place,
We'll stay on the course and fix our eyes on Your face.

# Mercy Anew

*"because of the Lord's great love, we are not consumed, for His mercies never fail. They are new every morning." Lam. 3:22-23*

It seemed my world closed in today, I felt so all alone,
I wandered in my desperate state
and turned my face toward "home".
Tears streaming down, throat aching deep,
I gulped a breath to plead, to wallow, cry and scream,
I felt the faintest dusting, a fine mist, no eye could see,
and as it fell upon me,
His voice rang with my heart's harmony:

"My child, my mercy's falling to rest on you today –
I give my strength when you falter
to lift you up from life's slippery clay.
Put your hand in my nail-pierced hand
and I promise, I'll lead the way.
Trust me when your eyes are blind
and keep step with me by My side.
I'll never leave you nor forsake you,
I'll be with you through this day.
So My mercies are fresh for your needs you confess, they fall like fresh
morning dew. Just turn your face toward heaven
as they fall each day on you."

His presence wrapped around me,
His love entwined my heart,
I knew that I could make it,
His mercy claimed each part.
I fell down on my knees,
ashamed, to say the least,
as I realized that His mercy
was the reason for His grace.

# What Choice Will You Make?

Sometimes we wish for fairy dust
to land and make things right,
we'd rather see the things we trust
than walk by faith, not sight,
and then when out upon a limb
we hear it crack and break,
no longer trust in God above
His name we do forsake.

Why do we place our faith in sight
to know each step we take?
When Abram walked into the night
God called, make no mistake,
he had no road map and no clue
God lead him day by day
he was one of the chosen few,
he believed while on the way.

Believing God seems very easy
when our faith is not involved,
the greater question then becomes,
Can I trust Him when I fall
or will I go on my own way
unbelieving all the while?
Just over the ridge, if only we'll stay,
our Promise Land does stretch for miles!

# He Set Me Free

For Doug

A night so lonely, dark and drear
it squeezed my heart with starkest fear,
cold fingers pierced, ripped through my soul
left dying, bleeding, my plight unknown.

I'd burned my bridges, every one,
no evil thing was left undone,
my albatross around my neck,
I couldn't see my life, a wreck.

And when life seemed to be its worst
it took a turn, became a curse,
and everything so dear to me,
was taken, and now I am no longer free.

Confusion tore my mind apart
insanity threatened to then resort,
playing games inside my head
I fell into the pit instead,

The pit coal black, I couldn't see
I scratched and clawed with no relief,
no sign of savior, friend or foe,
with nothing left, I finally broke.

Confession poured from lips unclean,
to whom I spoke, He was unseen
but my last hour of life, I thought,
if God is there, His mercy, I sought.

With gasping breath, and failing heart,
my eyes were opened to see darkness part,
His nail-pierced hand reached down, took hold,
to pull me up, to make me whole.

His healing hand stretched over me
He loosed my chains to set me free,
to walk beside him and to stay
close by His side, and not to stray.

He saved me not just from my sins,
He gave new life only found in Him
there will be many trials to come
but I'll walk the road behind the Son.

And if my life is not my own
I'll trust Him 'til my days are done
and then I'll rest eternally
because in the pit, He set me free!!!

# A Cord of Three

Dedicated to Robert and Ladell Smith and Samuel
Based on Ecc. 4:12


"A cord of three strands is not quickly broken"
as in Your word so long ago spoken
expectantly waiting what You had in store
Your hand touched our lives and now there are four.

So many heartaches, wrong roads, a broad path,
one soul was lost, doomed for eternal death.
The other was struggling a foothold to gain
as freewill would have it, broken and slain.

Pierced there and bleeding, His life given up
so as one day, the sacrificial cup.
Jesus took, He drank and poured out His life,
so Ladell could be saved, from darkness to light.

Two separate cords brought together from pain
from brokenness and sorrow, healing was gained.
Two became three, their lives vowed before God
cords bound forever and sealed from above.

Before time began, Jesus spoke into being
the time and the season for you to conceive,
a son placed within you, this promise He gave,
this cord of three strands came to seek and to save.

# Spirit-Soaring

Dedicated to Dave and Cheryl Dodson


Soaring as the eagles
Majestic wings unfurled
The tilting of earth's axis
The rushing wind does swirl
All about me gathers,
Land and sea to stretch for miles
Up there, time doesn't matter
I can release my earthly trials.

I gain a new perspective
Through God's eyes, I look to see,
His light shines down reflecting
All the valleys He's taken me
The rugged rocks and crooks and turns
Steep hills and deep ravines,
It was in the valley that I could learn
Without soaring, I couldn't see.

The times in life the way was broad
then sheer cliff, I tumbled down,
I lay there in a broken mess,
For I had traveled west.
I saw so clearly ruts and holes
Soaring far above the plane,
My eyes were opened, God's heart to know
An insight freshly gained.

The rugged way seemed never-ending
I thought it would surely go for miles
But just over the mountain spreading,
A lush, fertile valley for those bone-tired.
I looked across at a crystal sea,

I was drawn by its purity.
I cupped my hand and drank my fill,
Content, I lay there quiet and still.

No thought I gave to time or space
Broken and bruised, my heart just ached,
So unaware of that peaceful place
Earths trials upon me weighed
Just then, caught up in arms so strong
A healing balm to my soul applied
This was God's plan for me all along,
Jesus' mercy to me supplied.

This life will try to beat you down
When you can't see above the plane,
Soar above the barrier of sound
You can see the cross, blood-stained.
For in the Spirit where eyes can't see,
Flesh is yielded, you can go,
A place where peace and rest receive
A place where Jesus can make you whole!

# To Sarah

*Happy Birthday Sarah!*


On this your 18<sup>th</sup> birthday,
all that's in my heart, I'll say
Mel and I are so proud of you,
We ask God's blessings to fall anew.

As day after day comes and goes,
We pray heaven's wisdom you will know
and walk with Him life's narrow way
within His will, we hope you'll stay.

When life tries to beat you down,
It seems trials around you abound,
Hold on to Jesus, He is true,
Walk in His footsteps, His way is sure.

And as the future is coming near,
His voice will guide you as you hear,
Him directing every step
Ask Him to keep your heart in check.

He plans your future bright and true
Before you were born, this He knew,
You are so precious in His sight,
As you go forward, be His Light!

# Beside Quiet Waters

Dedicated to Dorothy Jean


Lush fertile crescent,
endless water supply,
strong oak from heaven to earth bent
there's nothing I need to rely.

I kept within my open space
I had no reason for time or place,
everything perfect within my sphere
no need to travel on from here.

The busyness of life trudged on
the lush green turned to brown
the water dried up with the dawn
the strong oak had been stripped down.

My perfect world fell all around me
I collapsed into a heap,
Forced to stop, to look and see,
My mind was opened to perceive.

This was not the chosen way
But one I took in self-reliance,
As it broadened, I continued to stay
I stumbled on in blind defiance.

In my weakness, I understood,
He allowed my wilderness wandering,
For in my rebellion, my sin He took
The price it cost to purchase me.

He gave His best and took my worst
His blood poured out on that Calvary hill,
His focus was God's kingdom first,
On my behalf, He would appeal.

He wants only His best for me,
He proved His love on that rugged tree,
So within His will, I must rely,
Trusting in myself, I must deny.

The cost too great to compromise,
Jesus paid it all that day,
My will and flesh must be crucified,
If I want to walk in His way.

Then He will lead me in green pastures,
And beside quiet waters, I'll stay,
When I trust Him in full measure
His hope and healing will come without delay!

# My Tender Savior

For Jennifer with love


Sometimes the choices that we make
are out from under God's protection
when at the crossroads, left we take
we break God's heart, we bring separation.
As the road widens left and right,
God calls to our hearts, "please return"
We keep stumbling on by sight
God's hand removed so we will learn.
His way will not on us be thrust
He gently calls and woos our hearts
Our choice is then on Him to trust
going His way is where repentance starts.
He is such a tender Savior, He is always a merciful Lord
before the Father, pleading our favor
our sin placed on Him, He could afford.
He awaits you Jen to place your hand
He loves you beyond earthly measure.
There's nothing you can do, He always understands
There waits for you heavenly treasure.
His arms are open wide, run straight into them,
He can take all the wrong and make it right,
His love will never put you down or condemn
He knows your songs in the night.
Trust in the Lord with all your heart
lean on Him not your own understanding
in His strength make this a new start
obeying Him, do what He commands.
He longs to give you so much more
He longs to pour out His favor,
Take the key, unlock the door
Be all He created you for.

# *Her Name is Rejoice*

Dedicated to Ms. Margie McCarley

There's a rumbling in the heavens
lightning streaks across the sky
all creation stands to echo
the earth shakes in sweet reply:

"Rejoice!  Her name is Rejoice!"

All around the birds chatter
the wind rocks in jubilee
keeping rhythm with the Master
the name rings out so happily:

"Rejoice!  Her name is Rejoice!"

I feel my spirit lifting
to heights I've never known
every fiber trembling
as I'm drawn up to His throne.

A joy beyond my reason
His splendor there adorned
with love that's never ceasing
a name hidden is now made known.

"O Daughter, your name is Rejoice!"

I shout in jubilation!
Hands raised, my feet respond,
I dance in sweet elation
Now, my spirit knows the song.

# City on a Hill

For Rhonda Buckingham, with love


My minds seeks out the question
I cannot understand,
the purpose of my existence
is there a grander plan?

When darkness presses o'er me,
no brightness in my day
inside I burst to be free
I long to run and play.

How did I end up in this place?
I grow up wondering,
then I met Jesus face to face
no longer blind, now I can see.

Before I existed, Your eyes saw me
a lump of unformed clay
precious hands from eternity,
molded me on that day.

I realized at that moment
amid darkness Your Light shines
not only for my enjoyment
but those in darkness, the truth to find.

I am a city on a hill,
shining out so brightly,
to family and friends but greater still
that they'll choose You for all eternity.

# The Essence of Ashley

To Ima with love
*In loving memory of Ashley Nicole Wright Walker*


The essence of Ashley is like fresh morning dew,
Dripping like honey, each day fresh and new,
Meeting the world with a smile big and wide,
Seeing each day as opportunity yet tried.

Such innocence she carried, too trusting at times.
She gave all she had even to her last dime.
A heart of gold, she listened, and gave her advice
If a friend was in need, she would self-sacrifice.

Her life was a gift sent from above
A sweet fragrance so lively, deep was her love
Though life was a struggle, she never gave up
Through months of darkness when times became tough.

Such beauty she had inside and out
Blinded by circumstance to God's goodness throughout
She sought to be loved for all that she was
God was waiting to hold her and fulfill all her trust.

Weary, this life all its evils and ills
Took hold of Ashley, intending to steal
But God in His mercy came like a white Knight,
To love her, to hold her, in eternity's light.

# To My Best Friend

Dedicated to Ladell Smith

I'd searched the whole world over
to find a friend a so true
God heard my prayer with tender care
and then He sent me you.

Amidst trials and tribulations,
sometimes deep defeat,
God spoke in divine supplication
through our friendship so complete.

Many times, I've wanted to give up
and leave this world behind,
but God intervened with a friends love
that could only have been divine.

I know you would say you haven't done much
but believe me, it's so much more
for the love of a TRUE friend goes down deep
where two hearts can beat as one.

I call you my best friend
I've searched for years, no one has ever stayed.
Today, I'm overwhelmed and I just had to say
Thanks, Ladell, for being that ONE.

# With All My Heart

To my Mom, with love


A special seed was planted
many years ago
sometimes she took for granted
how the nurturing hand did show

Through adversity, drought and famine
somehow the seed grew on
to become the slightest image
of her mother's seed bestowed.

With a thankful heart, I want to be
everything you've shown to me
beauty, grace, compassion, prove
a mother's heart of love is true.

Today, I honor all you are
and what you are to me
when God breathed life into your soul
a daughter's heart was then made whole.

# My Lily in the Valley

Dedicated to Nora Sifuentes, with love


The fairest of ten thousand
My sweet Nora, you are to Me,
you are My Lily in the Valley
a sweet fragrance so beautiful to see.

I chose you for this appointed time,
I placed and planted you so rare,
I crafted you with hand divine
So that, My Love, none can compare.

I love you beyond distraction
Your beauty matches inside and out,
With tenderness, My hand out stretches
To prune and cut, but have no doubt,

Your splendor far surpasses
What I had in mind for you to be
For Nora, when I look at you,
Your beauty shines, reflecting Me!

# My Vessel of Honor

For Darrel


A broken vessel, there you sat
you felt worthless, of no use in fact,
no one could love someone like me
nowhere to turn, you longed to be free.
Headstrong you ran, life used you up,
Then thrown away, caught in a trap.

That's where He found you,
picked up the clay,
rest in His hands, forever stay
a vessel of honor, so lovely to see
taken from the deepest mire, the dirtiest pit
that's when He works best and makes you fit.

He never throws the clay away
that's why He chose the price to pay
the costliest vessels
come from the deepest mire
His most prized possessions
Because they've gone through the fire.

# *Can You Open Your Heart?*

Should I write of hearts and flowers
of pretty things and the Eiffel Tower?
Of days long past, a note left on the door
To pleasure awaiting with more in store?
Or times of stolen kisses beneath
The mistletoe and evergreen wreath?
Those days are long past said goodbye
And that silly girl, has long past died.

The woman I am is broken and used
Not sure, for the future seems aloof and confused
Wanting and needing to be cherished and loved
Not really ready with all that I've lost.
My heart is so numb, lifeless and cold,
It beats, but I feel nothing at all.

I don't want to cause any hurt or pain,
Everything's jumbled, nothings the same
Every moment cries life's unfair
Warped and twisted, sometimes despair
How do I let go and move on?
When it seems all that's good is gone?
What do you want?  Can you reach out in pain?
Can in the ashes of grief and shame
Build something new, open your heart once again?
For the pathway to love is paved with friendships hand.

# What Will You Choose?

For Doug

Encased inside this glass of pain,
nowhere to hide, I wear my shame
naked before the world to see,
I long to just be free.

It is my hand that locked the door
my penance – years and life destroyed
nothing I felt left to redeem
My life a waste in total defeat.

With nothing I felt left to lose,
A light shone, a path to choose,
Will I allow my chains to drop?
Overcome my pain, the fear to stop?

Will I take a risk, reach out my hand?
Will I take a step of faith and stand?
Upon the solid rock, I know?
Cast satan out, walk in the unknown?

What would Jesus have me do?
Is fear from Him or is He true?
Will He ever lead me wrong?
Can I depend on Him, be strong?

This is for you, Doug, what will you do?
The path of light, will this you choose?
Or will you stay in darkness bound?
His hand reached out, will you be found?

# *Valley Of Delights*

December 6<sup>th</sup>, 2008
*In Memory of Mel Rowell*


God took my hand and led me into
the darkest valley I've ever seen
I left behind the life I knew
to what I call "in between"
the old life passed before my eyes,
the more we walked, the deeper it came
I realized it was death's valley
and that things would never be the same.

My strength it failed, my legs gave way
a burden so heavy, my spirit was enslaved,
weighted down, my sin disguised,
completely hopeless, I felt despised.
My pain and grief, all I had lost
was all my eyes could see
the darkest night, the deepest valley,
I cried, my heart a plea.

Just then, a shaft of light poured down
revealing the path ahead,
a trap, a pit awaited me, Jesus led me on around.
He took the weight upon His shoulders,
it was nothing at all to Him
We walked in green pastures, the crystal waters still.
For my hungry, weary soul,
He prepared a table there before me
My spirit fed, no more enslaved,
I was once again set free.

As valleys come and they surely will,
take My hand, let your heart be still
for the road is rough, the way is steep
if you'll walk beside me, your soul, I'll keep.
For in this valley of death and loss
It leads straight down from the cross,
Because in the heart of this dark valley lies,
My purest river called Delights.

Not everyone can walk there
It is for the darkest times I share,
The very core of who I AM
My mercy and grace abundant, none compares.
So when you face the valley of decision,
When all hope seems lost with no provision,
Remember, I walked, my footsteps stay
For is this valley is THE WAY.

# About the Author:

Pam Rowell-Scoggins lives in Texas and is remarried after the death of her husband. She has been writing poetry off and on since 1979. Back in 1997 after a long period of not writing, Pam wrote a poem for her grandmother's 80th birthday celebration. Since then, her poetry is inspired by people in her life who are going through different seasons of their lives. All the dedicated poems are those written by inspiration from God. She enjoys writing and most definitely helping people. She is working toward her counseling degree.